C000230237

Robin Green worked as a priest in the Church of England in locations as varied as Mirror Group Newspapers and a society church in Kensington. He resigned in 1990 over issues of sexual orientation; with his partner Ralph he developed an aromatherapy business in south London. They now live in Deal in Kent.

For Ruth and Kirsten and my partner, Ralph.

Robin Green

TALES FROM THE CRYPT:

A LIFE IN AND OUT OF THE CHURCH

AUSTIN MACAULEY
PUBLISHERS LTD.

A CIP catalogue record for this title is available from the British Library.

ISBN 9781786292315 (Paperback)
ISBN 9781786292322 (Hardback)
ISBN 9781786292339 (eBook)
www.austinmacauley.com

First Published (2017)
Austin Macauley Publishers Ltd.
25 Canada Square
Canary Wharf
London
E14 5LQ

Contents

PROLOGUE

Penelope Lively in her memoir *Ammonites and Leaping Fish* writes about the emergence of old age and comments: "We simply get more like ourselves." This book, written at the beginning of my seventh decade, tests the truth of that hypothesis. In the age of the selfie and a culture based on the cult of celebrity how do we assess the reality of our own lives without self-indulgence and self-deception? Autobiography rarely avoids those pitfalls and I know I will fall prey to both in the writing of this book. But that does not distract from that compulsion on the brink of old age to understand and form a narrative that validates the struggles, pain and excitement of seventy years of self-discovery. Is there a signature identity that weaves together the multiple strands of trying to live honestly through the traumas and opportunities of the second half of the twentieth century and the beginning of the twenty-first? All of us can bear witness to what we have seen.

It is not a coincidence that titles of popular songs or a play on those titles are the chapter headings. There are two social movements that have formed my social and cultural understanding of the years through which I have lived. They are the consumer society and popular music. Those two forces have shaped much of Britain's understanding of itself in the last sixty years and remain, more especially in the age of the Internet, the dominant cultural influences of our time. Many of my friends will be puzzled by my choice of musical titles. They know that not only am I tone deaf but also the least musical of people. They would not feature here at all if I had not known Ralph, my beloved partner. Music is central to his life and most of the time forms the background to our lives. Among the numerous gifts he has given me over most of the last thirty years is an appreciation of the popular music of the seven decades of my life.

Centuries ago Sir Thomas Browne wrote about a human life as "the varieties of himself". My life has not had a straightforward trajectory. It has finished up down blind alleys more than once. It has taken me from the cloying small-town life of Suffolk to the edges of Madagascar. I have travelled through at least three different careers and they have brought me face to face with some of the poorest people in the world. I have also confronted some of the richest and I have no illusions about which I prefer. When I was the parish priest at St Mary the Boltons in south Kensington a sheikh from the Middle East offered me half a million pounds to stop ringing the church bell on Sundays. It was waking up the harem and eunuchs! I have no illusions about the power of money and the ways in which it distorts our view of the world. The varieties of myself led me down the blind alley of heterosexual marriage but also into the freedom and exhilaration of being a gay man. That in turn posed crises for me as an ordained priest and forced new explorations and new adventures. I will never quite understand how at the end of six decades Ralph and I finished up in another small town, this time in Kent. But we did and all the ambivalence I feel about that is the context in which this book is now being written.

Within two years of my birth the world was overshadowed by the horrors of Hiroshima and Nagasaki. As a student in Leeds I remember that night in 1962 when we all huddled together for fear that the Cuba crisis would plunge the world into nuclear suicide. It was a period too dominated by the deaths of John Kennedy and Martin Luther King. Our dreams seemed to die very fast. From Kosovo to Iraq and Afghanistan my lifetime has been shaped by hideous, and often deeply misguided, military conflicts. It is said that we are the accretion of all that we have been. We are also the accretion of all that has happened in the course of a lifetime. It has shaped our values, our political perspectives, and our world view. Psychology would sometimes have us believe that we are primarily shaped by the earliest childhood experiences. Whilst not wanting to deny that it seems to me that life is much more complex than that, the world, the societies in which we live also play a fundamental part in the ways we understand ourselves and the world. The "varieties of himself" also tell a story about the history of the world in a single lifetime. The political and the personal are threads in a single narrative.

The places we live in, the houses we have inhabited and the possessions with which we surround ourselves all tell part of our story. Gardens and allotments, pictures and sculptures, bookcases stuffed with a lifetime's reading, boxes filled with vinyl and CDs all tell you something about a human life. Yet as important as any of that is I don't believe that they have been central to my narrative. That is why I have called this book *Tales from the Crypt*. It is my engagement with other people that has been at the root of the formation of myself. The time I spent in my early twenties working with young heroin addicts in central London was the most formative period of the last seventy years and that is why I start my story there. The 1960s was the decade that shaped my generation: both its exhilaration and its darkness brought us alive as human beings after the dullness and narrow vision of the post-War period. It was the foundation stone on which I built the rest of my life. All the other tales have their origin there.

CHAPTER ONE

LIVING ON THE DARK
SIDE OF THE MOON

"Was it for this that the clay grew tall?"

(Wilfred Owen)

It was June 1967 and the telephone rang in the
Cambridge college where I had just discovered my
Theology Tripos result. "Norman Houses here, Robin.
Forget coming to us for your vacation work. Someone
else needs you much more." I was due to spend my
summer vacation working in one of the Norman Houses,
halfway places for prisoners who had recently been
discharged. The director of them told me that he had just
had a phone call from the Vicar of St Martin-in-the-
Fields in Trafalgar Square. He had a crisis on his hands.

In the early months of 1967 a large group of young,
and predominantly homeless, young people had invaded

the National Gallery in Trafalgar Square and were causing significant disruption to the Gallery's day-to-day life. For the first time in its history the Gallery had employed security staff and the group of young people had been banned. They had walked across the road and taken over the church of St Martin-in-the-Fields.

St Martin's had a long and honourable tradition of caring for homeless men and women. Their Social Services Unit was a leader in providing support, both mental and physical, mainly to people who were heavily dependent on alcohol and had no known address. During the first and second world wars the church's crypt had acted as a shelter for people in central London. A previous vicar, Dick Sheppard, had a national reputation as someone who embodied a vision of the Church as an inclusive community free of bigotry and exclusiveness. However the crypt had closed in 1947 and all the work was done through the Social Services Unit.

The group of young people posed a new problem. Apart from finding them sleeping, and usually sleeping together, under the altar, hypodermic syringes were scattered in the pews. In the decade before trafficked drugs slowly became a part of the national consciousness this was a phenomenon rarely seen in central London let alone other parts of England. The Church of England was largely trapped in a middle-class, and middle-aged, bubble oblivious to many of the sea changes that were convulsing Europe and most of the 'Western' world. Nowhere typified that better than the claustrophobic theological college in Cambridge where I had spent the last two years. Most of my fellow students were products of the public school system and most of what we were taught was completely unconnected to the realities of everyday life.

Austen Williams, the charismatic Vicar of St Martin's, had taken the courageous decision to reopen the crypt after twenty years and to encourage the group of young people to use it as daytime refuge. His problem was that he had no staff resources to run it. That is where I came in. This felt like a huge breath of fresh air after the suffocating and irrelevant syllabi that I had suffered from for two years. I hurried to central London and knew within five minutes that I wanted to work with this ecclesiastical giant. I knew that I would have to return to Cambridge at some point to finish my studies but, for the time being, I could really discover what it meant to be a priest.

Between 1960 and 1964 the number of heroin addicts known to the Home Office rose from ninety-four to 342. By 1970 2657 addicts were notified. By 1992 24,703 addicts were on the Home Office lists. Those figures alone give some indication of the escalation in the problem. The later figures are, of course, indicative of the advent of trafficked drugs from other parts of the world, a phenomenon that began in the late 1970s. Back in 1967 the problem was largely confined to central London although well-heeled suburbs like Kingston on Thames already had small pockets of addicts.

National government had recognised that there was an issue and had set up the Interdepartmental Committee on Drug Addiction chaired by Lord Brain, a former President of the Royal College of Physicians. In its first report in 1961 it had proposed medical responses to the problem. Up until that time it had been regarded as a criminal issue. This was a debate that was to erupt again and again for the next fifty years. The first report identified drug dependency as primarily a mental issue and saw the route to its solution through psychiatric units. That view was reinforced in the 1965 second report, "the addict should be regarded as a sick person [and] should be treated as such and not as a criminal, provided that he does not resort to criminal acts."

Since the 1920s there had been very little opiate addiction. It had tended to be 'therapeutic addicts' whose dependence had grown through medical treatments and that meant that by the 1960s this was largely a diminishing and elderly population. The Brain Committee recognised that both the social and age demographic was changing. It was, said the Committee, a "socially infectious condition". The Brain Committee in response to this formulated a model of care that recognised addiction as a medical illness but one that needed to be pursued within a public health approach. As a result of the report's recommendations the 1967 Dangerous Drugs Act and the 1968 Dangerous Drugs Regulations were formulated.

Although Whitehall and the arches under Charing Cross were yards apart, government regulations meant little to the young people I began to know in the crypt underneath St Martin's. It was, in many senses of the word, an underworld. The main sources of support were not psychiatric clinics but a ragbag community of bright and intelligent, damaged and crucified, vibrant and desperate, young people. I realised very quickly that what I had to do was to create a place of belonging and trust and then to find out what was causing the patterns of behaviour in this highly vulnerable group of people.

The second report of the Brain Committee in 1965 had another conclusion. The new group of addicts' addiction was fed not by trafficked drugs but "the activity of a very few doctors who have prescribed excessively for addicts". The same thing took another form for me. I was regularly being asked for a fiver. (My weekly wages were £6 although St Martins gave me a room to live in.) One of the cardinal principles when working with homeless people is that you do not do financial handouts. So no fivers were forthcoming. But I began to recognise that the overprescribing of heroin, and to a minor degree cocaine, was one of the primary engines of the young people's addiction

This was confirmed by none other than the *Daily Mail* and the *Sun*! Media reports began to appear about the activities of a Dr John Petro. In 1967 the General Medical Council had begun to act against the private practitioner based on reports that he was prescribing in London's Underground stations and in other public places. They erased him from the Register after the Home Secretary had withdrawn his powers to prescribe 'dangerous drugs'. Clearly Petro was not the only practitioner indulging in this activity. In the decades following one of the main tensions in the field of the treatment of drug addiction was that between the mainstream medical profession and the private practitioners.

Petro was, of course, much closer to the young people I was working with than official government committees. But the Brain Committee's recommendation was to lead by the late 1960s to the first major public health intervention. Between 1968 and 1970 hospital-based drug dependency units were set up and heroin and cocaine licences were mainly confined to the psychiatric staff working in these units. It was these units that had a transforming effect on the lives of many of the young people that I saw. Instead of being trafficked illegal drugs in Charing Cross Station their illness was being

19

managed within a medical framework. It was part of my job to help them make the transition from the underworld to a world of safer sanity.

I was not alone in that work. Despite the Brain Committee's overall view most of the young people I knew indulged in some form of petty crime. One of my allies was the first Afro-Caribbean officer to be appointed to the Metropolitan Police. Like me, he was an outsider and both of us had an empathy with these kids from the edge. We knew something of the mental, physical and sexual abuse they had suffered from. But more importantly we knew what it was to be an outsider. At the time I had no idea where that came from for me. Over the next fifty years I was to discover that being gay was a beautiful human gift. Another of my allies was Jeanne Townsend who volunteered to help. Jeanne had all the quirky bohemian traits that helped her comprehend the young people at a deep level. After we both left she wrote to me from Kenya. I shall always cherish her words: 'Robin what you created was a miracle of trust'.

When I reflect on that time I recognise a discovery that has served me well in public life over the years. To be a public servant is to be a private detective. Both in my working life and in retirement I have had to engage with government at all levels. I know that no form of government yields truth easily. It is often hidden away in Appendix 4 of a report that nobody bothers to read. My gradual realisation that it was illicit medical practitioners overprescribing, and overcharging for, drug supplies that taught me this valuable lesson. I had not read the Brain report but by living daily alongside the young people and building trust with them I had discovered what was one of the sources of their addictive behaviour. That in turn could lead to a change in public policy that addressed the root causes of the issue and developed strategies to deal with it.

When the time came to leave and hand over the work to a brilliant pair of radical Salvation Army officers I wrote:

"[I]t is part, and only part, of the story of a generation which is different – different in its values, in its self-confidence, its way of observing the world. In one way its roots are very much in the past, insofar as it has been conditioned by the traditions and culture of this country; but as it looks to the future it sees little more than the prospect of a universal Hiroshima: and it is the broken part of this group, which in its pilgrimage of despair has set up its home in the Crypt."

And then I continued:

"We should have a new vision of what it is to be human in the 20th century and an explosion of the life of Christ into the heart of London and the needs of both young and old..."

I have begun my memoir here because it holds so many of the clues to what has shaped my life, mind and heart throughout my adult life. Some of that has been spent in the institutional Church but a lot has also been on the edges of that and beyond. Inevitably some people ask me what I think the word God means. If it means anything at all it is the beloved presence among a fractured and expectant humanity. The Word was made flesh: the Church spends its life turning the flesh into words. God is nothing unless understood as a presence creating a miracle of trust in the underworlds of this world.

I know it is a platitude but people matter above all else. To know the depths of your being and to be the person you truly are is the human right of every person. Secular and ecclesiastical bodies too often use policy and theology to override what enables people to live in community free from bigotry and hostile prejudice. Nowhere has that been truer than in the opening years of the twenty-first century. A lot of politics and a lot of faith practice have lost sight of that reality in the relentless pursuit of austerity and rigid morality. I shall always be grateful to a senior magistrate at Bow Street magistrates' court. Anna was up for the very minor offence of stealing a pint of milk. The magistrate said: "This young woman has been abused, raped and despised all her life. Her father locked her in an attic for days on end and at one point nailed up the door. I am committing her into the care of St Martins. She has told me that it is the only place she will ever feel safe." "We are put on earth for a little space that we might learn to bear the beams of love." (William Blake) It was in that underworld in 1967 that I began to glimpse what that might mean. But where had I been before that?

CHAPTER TWO

STRANGER ON THE SHORE

"Man needs difficulties; they are necessary for health."

(Carl Jung)

A ten-year-old boy walks through the dark streets of Sudbury in Suffolk with the family spaniel, Judy. It is late afternoon on Christmas Day 1953. As he gazes through the windows lit with fairy lights he senses that he is alone. That boy was me and it was the first time I really sensed what it meant to be an outsider. The nation was anticipating a new Elizabethan era full of optimism and hope after the grim years of Depression and the Second World War. I was facing the daunting prospect of the dreaded Eleven Plus exam with all the parental expectations that went with it in this new surge of social hope for the nation. That sense of being the outsider was never to leave me but mercifully the teenage angst was later transformed into a resource for health and life.

Dogs play a big part in my story. Judy was no exception. At this moment of realisation she was my companion, the one who shared the pain. Ten years later I was listening to an American woman theologian in Great St Mary's Cambridge expound the thesis that "God is Dog and Dog is God." She was part of the crazy and exhilarating theological debate that was to convulse the Church of England in the 1960s. But despite the craziness, part of my reality is that dogs have always mediated to me a sense of unconditional love. They have always been there for me.

Julian Clary once said that one of the saddest things about life is that dogs live such a short time compared with humans. Graham Norton in a recent autobiography writes of their companionship and significance. Paul O'Grady regularly appears on television pleading the cause of neglected and abandoned dogs. Perhaps it is no coincidence that we are all gay men and the desire for an unconditional love has been fired by all the remnants of homophobia in British society. Certainly that experience on Christmas Day 1953 was my first unconscious recognition of being different. I was not the same as my brother and sisters back in the family home enjoying the final joys of Christmas Day. Sixty years later Mr Ross enriches the lives of my partner, Ralph, and me, the latest in companions stretching back through the decades.

So who was that family waiting at home on that Christmas Day? Joan, my mother was a formidable woman. She also kept secrets close to her ample bosom. It wasn't until 1990 that I discovered she was a bastard and the beloved grandparents who I adored were in fact her adopted parents. Her real mother turned out to be Great Aunt Nell, my 'grandfather's' youngest sister. In 1920 Nell was living with a married man, William Hinchcliff, in Bromley in Kent. Although not married she called herself Nell Hinchcliff on my mother's birth certificate. In 1921 Nell and William had another daughter and it seems likely that it was then that my mother was passed over to William, her brother, and his wife Flora. There is no evidence of any formal adoption. It happened then.

Forty-nine years later in 1969 Nell went with her sister Elizabeth Mowll to the Registrar General's office and swore statuary declarations. She changed her name back to the family name of Major, removed William Hinchcliff and his profession from the birth certificate and also removed Hinchcliff's place of residence. Whether my mother knew anything about this I shall never know. I don't even know if she knew she was adopted. But much of her behaviour suggested she knew or suspected something. She placed a disproportionate emphasis on outward appearance and always managed to avoid difficult conversations. I realise now that shame plays a big part in my family story.

We were not well off back in the 1950s and I was often used to fend off the creditors. I can remember all too vividly times when the family larder at our house in Sudbury was bare. When the bakery lady came round in her van I would be sent out to fend her off for another day. To this day I have a horror of wasted food but more importantly I recognise an inner terror that somebody might expose something about me. Being the good boy was fed by this dysfunctional family dynamic. In family therapy we know that the whole often offers the clue to some form of mental or emotional disorder in individual members of the family. Outward appearance and responsibility are part of my family legacy. When I was thirteen my mother had to have a hysterectomy. In those days the convalescence took ten weeks. I was expected to run the family home, prepare the meals for a father and four brothers and sisters and also go to school fulltime. By this time my father was also a funeral director and I was left to manage phone calls from grieving people. It is no wonder that for most of my adult life I have felt over responsible and terrified that failure would plunge me into shame.

But that is not the whole story. We are beginning to recognise the truth of Jung's insight. Difficulties are what help underdogs to excel. They are desirable difficulties, a useful form of pragmatism. My mother was also the queen of flower arranging in East Anglia in the 1950s. She fed my passion for gardening and plants and natural beauty. My father, who I will come to later, also had a passion for growing roses. That passion was passed on to me. I became the teenage toy boy of the East Anglian ladies who were developing this art and which was spawning flower clubs all over Britain. This came to a climax in 1956 when the Chelsea Flower Show created a flower arranging marquee for the first time.

East Anglia nominated me as one of their representatives. The Royal Horticultural Society mandarins were not amused. How could a thirteen-year-old boy possibly be an exhibitor, probably at that time the youngest person ever to exhibit at the prestige show? But difficulties help underdogs to excel and after a battle the exhibitor's pass was issued. I went on to win awards at all the major East Anglian shows and eventually became the youngest judge in flower arranging in England. By the time that I was doing GCEs (the then term for GCSEs) my aspiration was to work for the Queen's florist, Moyses Stevens, in London. That nonsense was soon to be knocked out of me!

Long before Tony Blair uttered the mantra 'Education, education, education' my father, Bernard, was chanting. He came from a very austere lower middle class family that was awash with endless aunts and uncles. His father, William, was a tax collector and his wife, Rhoda, a dressmaker. William came from a large and sprawling Essex family and many of my childhood memories are about visiting endless aunts and uncles. Rhoda came from a small family in Boughton in Kent and had spent most of her early life in service as a ladies' maid. Bernard was their only child and at the age of twelve had suffered rheumatic fever, a disease which fatally affected his heart. The weakness was eventually to kill him. It also meant that he never served in the military in the Second World War. Instead he became the regulator of meat distribution in Essex and Suffolk. He was later to become a funeral director mainly for the Co-op.

William and Rhoda were lifelong supporters of the Labour Party but Bernard, in a rare act of rebellion, joined the Conservative Party and was eventually the agent for the Member of Parliament for West Suffolk, John Hare. He was also elected as a county councillor and later became the Chairman of the West Suffolk Education Committee. He was part of that aspirational movement in the 1950s, believing that education was the fundamental clue to human success. I was part of his experiment! As the oldest son the expectations were loaded on me. Neither my brother nor my sisters ever

27

experienced the same pressure. I scraped through the Eleven Plus and was immediately presented with the choice, grammar school or the local public school, Felstead. With very little self-confidence and lots of insecurity about who I was, I opted for the local grammar school. How he expected to meet public school fees I shall never understand!

Where I live in Kent debate still rages about the virtues of a grammar school system over comprehensive education. Kent still has grammar schools. I hated mine. For half my time there it was run by tyrants, the worst of whom was a brute called Colonel Anglebeck. He thought nothing of tearing pupils from their desks and booting them along the floor into the school corridor. There was an air of physical and mental brutality in the place only balanced by a handful of benign and intelligent masters. All this changed when halfway through my time a completely new kind of educator, Mr Strachan, was appointed. The ethos in the school, whilst still retaining some of its more dubious traditions, changed. But the Army Cadet Corps did not go. It was my first act of teenage rebellion and parental disobedience. I resolutely refused to have anything to do with its pseudo-militarism. Fortunately Mr Strachan recognised a reality, that I probably didn't, and told me to spend the time reading poetry in the library.

So my education was about overcoming insecurity and humiliation. My father's chairmanship of the Education committee did not help. For the whole of the first five years I was kept in the B stream of the school. This was brought to a head when we were doing mock GCEs. I scored 98% for my English Language essay *The River*. My English teacher told the whole school that I had outstripped every student in the A stream. But I was still relegated to the B stream. The teachers particularly hated my father's belief in changing to a four-term school year the idea of which they abhorred. I was punished for it.

But again difficulties served the underdog well. I gained nine GCEs even passing Maths, algebra in particular passing my comprehension. I went on to the sixth form but even here I was dogged by a regime determined not to nurture and encourage ability. When the time came to decide a future Anglebeck told me I was only fit for teacher training college and that university was out of the question. I rebelled, getting three good A levels and admission to the University of Leeds. I fulfilled my father's dreams. I got a top second in English Literature and Fine Art. Later on at the University of Cambridge I gained a top second in Theology Perhaps I was learning that it was better to be a big fish in a small pond rather than a small fish in a big pond. There are advantages to being the outsider in a marginal world. It turns out not to be a disadvantage after all. Underdogs excel by embracing difficulties. They turn out to be desirable.

It is a truism but look at any person and to some extent you see the parents. I know that is true of me. However much I resented my father's aspiration I know that he helped release the natural intelligence that I possess. He also gave me a model of public and political service which has served me well throughout the whole of my adult life. Although I hated the form it took I know that public service is the keystone of a democratic and civil society. Numerous communities today only survive because of the dedication and hard work of volunteers who enrich our world beyond any kind of human measurement. My mother either lived a life of denial or was it a struggle to overcome early difficulty? I will never know but what I do know is that she taught me, probably unintentionally, that difficulties are the energy that in the end nurtures self-confidence and self-respect. They never seem like a gift from heaven but the deeper reality is that they are an endowment for the future.

You can never escape being the 'stranger on the shore', a piece of music that haunted me during the early years of my life and still brings tears to my eyes today. As my great friend, Paul Ellison, a professor of music in San Francisco would gently remind me, "music can touch depths of being that nothing else can." But what my early life taught me was that being the outsider grants you a position of great privilege. The outsider is given a place where sometimes it is possible to see more clearly the social realities of a world that is too often fractured by bigotry, moral blindness and self-deception. In her wonderful book about the last years of living with terminal cancer Kate Gross writes:

"The dots that really matter aren't the ones you decide you want to do, but how you want to be." (Late Fragments)

Perhaps that is the deepest clue to my early life. It was the opportunity to choose who I wanted to be. The reality was that there were to be many hiccups along the way.

CHAPTER THREE

A MAN WITH THE CHILD
IN HIS EYES

*"You are a priest. But you must never neglect the
oceans or the forests."*

(Man on a bench in Market Street, San Francisco.)

It was a spring day in 1994 in San Francisco. It was my
second visit there and I was resting on a bench in one of
the city's main streets. A guy approached me and asked
if he could read my palm. Instantly suspicious I thought
he was after money. He denied it and said he had been
drawn to me. Nothing about my appearance told him
anything about my history. As soon as he opened my
hand he came out with the words with which this chapter
starts: "You are a priest." I was gobsmacked. How could
he possibly know? And could he understand the crisis
through which I had recently passed? As he continued to
read my palm I knew that he understood that priesthood

could exist way beyond the edges of the institutional church. Walking down Market Street twenty years later in 2015 I looked back with enormous gratitude to that man. He had affirmed me in a way that twenty-five years of institutional church life had failed to do.

My life in the Church of England had taken me from the poverty of the Elephant and Castle in south London to the multimillion-pound mansions of south Kensington via wealthy Surrey villages, the corridors of power in Mirror Group newspapers and the corridors of youthful ambition in the Roehampton Institute in south London. I had worked at all levels of the education system from opening one of the first preschool playgroups to teaching at university level. I had helped create a new form of university chaplaincy and had spent years developing the pastoral skills of women aspiring to play a part in the Church's life. I had served on the General Synod of the Church of England as a kind of ecclesiastical MP. Nobody could say that my twenty-five years spent in the Church of England wasn't varied. But the common narrative that runs through most of it was that I was on the fringes of traditional church life. There were good and not so good reasons for that. Those reasons were finally to knock me off the edge.

In 1969, a year after starting work as a curate at the Elephant and Castle, I had married Jean Woods, an ambitious young social worker. Five years later our twin daughters, Kirsten and Ruth, were born. It all ended in emotional chaos in 1980. I had to confront the eruption of a different sexual orientation. To this day the scars of that time still hurt. I know that I betrayed Jean and leaving her with two small children was an unforgiveable abandonment. I was in too deep emotional pain to understand what was happening. The truth is she brought up Ruth and Kirsten with great resilience and today both my daughters are outstanding human beings, happily married and working with autistic children and adults. I would like to think that they inherited my conviction that difficulties can be desirable and a source of emotional strength. For me the years that followed were a time of trying to heal the splits between desire and obligation, trust and suspicion and order and chaos. Divorce in 1980 certainly relegated me to the fringes of church life.

The 1960s are often written about as a time of sexual liberation and 1963, according to Phillip Larkin, was when sexual intercourse was invented. As I reflected earlier, for many people it was more like "living on the dark side of the moon". Gay relationships between adult men were only legalised in 1967, the year that I spent working at St Martin-in-the-Fields. There were virtually no role models for gay men and for thousands of us sexual discovery was a profoundly painful and difficult experience. It may sound crazy but in 1969 I had no conscious recognition of myself as a gay man. That came later and with devastating consequences. For years I have been intrigued at the ways self-deception functions in human growth and development. Yes, I was self–deceived, but it was not a conscious and intentional act.

This was, of course, made much worse by being part of the Church of England, an institution that continues in 2015 to be bedevilled in its attitudes to gay people. England, Alan Bennett has commented, is a deeply hypocritical country. We claim, for example, that London is one of the greatest cities on earth but day by day we sell it off to the Chinese and Russians! It is no wonder, therefore, that the Church of England is a deeply hypocritical institution. It claims to be an embracing place whilst at every turn it practises homophobia. In 1980 I was invited to contribute to a small volume of essays entitled *Prejudice and Pride*. The essays analysed the multitude of ways in which homophobia created hostile environments at many levels of British society. Much has been written about institutional racism but institutional homophobia was just as pervasive in the 1980s and 1990s and continues to a lesser degree, today.

In South London in the 1970s and 80s this was compounded by conspiracies in the centres of ecclesiastical power. The Bishop of Southwark at that time, Mervyn Stockwood, behaved like a prince bishop with an eye for every pretty young curate! When I discussed my divorce with other bishops there was a mute support but the message was clear: "Keep quiet about your sexuality and carry on having gay relationships. But under no circumstances live with anybody." Later in 1990 when the crisis came to a head I had a vigorous argument with Peter Selby, the then Bishop of Kingston. I wanted to resign because I was living with Ralph and could not square that with Church discipline. His attitude was: "You can't resign. You have done nothing wrong." To which my response was simply: "Make up your mind."

This strange ambivalence and confusion also persisted at other levels of Church life. When I was appointed in the 1980s to be the Vicar of St Mary the Boltons in wealthy South Kensington all hell broke loose. There had been a battle of power between the Bishop of Kensington and the lay people at the church about the appointment. A few lay people had advanced a preferred candidate but he was blacklisted in the diocese of London. So the bishop would not entertain his appointment. I was selected from a shortlist of eleven priests. It wasn't long before I received a phone call: "Duck for cover Robin. The *Sun* and the *News of the World* are after you." I went into hiding in my home in South London with my two daughters who I was looking after at the time. Reporters and photographers from both newspapers pursued me there, screaming through the letterbox: "You have abandoned your wife and children." A strange kind of abandonment when they could hear the children playing in the house! It transpired that three female members of the St Mary's congregation had phoned the papers with these vicious rumours. They included a senior lecturer at Imperial College, the widow of a Clerk to the House of Commons and the wife of an Anglican archdeacon.

Some weeks later I met with these three ladies to attempt some form of rapport. It became clear immediately that homophobia was parading behind the mask of opposition to divorced priests. I was faced with this: "You will be the Pied Piper of Earls Court attracting all kinds of queers and prostitutes and homeless people to our lovely church. We are in charge here and we will not tolerate the likes of you." I tried gently to say that Jesus seemed to me the eternal Pied Piper and what they had described was the kind of community he had envisioned. It was to little avail and for the next five years a quiet battle went on in the groves of Kensington about what the Church was really meant to be. If it had not been for lovely people like the Director of Music, Paul Ellison, lay women like Dorothy Patrick and Dorothy Coleman and ecclesiastical rogues like Archdeacon Tim Raphael I would not have survived five months.

The real crisis came in 1990. I was working for USPG a mission and aid agency in the Anglican Communion. It was an exciting appointment especially as I had responsibility for the Indian Ocean region and had met wonderful people from the Seychelles, Mauritius and Madagascar. This had culminated in an extraordinary pilgrimage of over 10,000 people to Lichfield Cathedral where we had a celebrated a day of what it meant to be truly human in an interdependent world. I had also met Ralph in 1987 and was living with him, as happy as I had ever been since leaving St Martins twenty years before.

During that time I would help out at the church of Saint John at Waterloo. It was there whilst I was celebrating a lunchtime Eucharist that the crunch came. In the middle of the main prayer I had a chronic anxiety attack and ground to a complete halt. I knew that my integrity was at stake. A few weeks later I tended my resignation. At the time George Carey was about to be made Archbishop of Canterbury and it was obvious that the Church of England was about to descend into a decade of deepening homophobia and the institutional persecution of gay people. I was told that his sole charge to a new Bishop of Southwark was: "Purge that diocese of all those queers". His appointment was to set the Church of England back fifty years. The ascendancy of the Evangelical wing of that church through the 1990s and into the twenty-first century has paralysed any attempts to make that Church a community of people free of prejudice and embracing all people irrespective of their origins, their ethnic background or their sexual orientation.

At its root are two things. The Evangelical wing whilst uplifting the importance of the biblical records in fact abuses them. Their biblical understanding of human sexuality is corrupt, relying on a few texts largely derived from the Jewish record and parroting these texts as though they are the final word on human sexual orientation. Much detailed analysis of the textual material has been done over the years. This large and influential group often disregard the substantial body of scholarship that has analysed those texts. Secondly Evangelicals with their emphasis on personal religion have a very weak sense of what the Church is. The result is a lack of any real awareness that communities can have a deeply transforming effect on people. They can be as I suggested earlier "a miracle of trust". When I worked in Kensington I prepared eight mature people for confirmation in the Church. The event took place at Holy Trinity Brompton. Afterwards over half the adults I had prepared said, "That was an infantile event: we were treated like tiny children." Evangelical religion often keeps people in a state of infantile dependence. Perhaps that is why it cannot deal with adult matters like sex!

For the last twenty-five years I have lived outside the confines of the institutional Church. That Church would not allow me to resign my priest's orders so a priest I remain. Or do I? I have asked myself that question many a time. In 1989 Ralph and I set up a business selling herbs and spices, aromatherapy and other natural products. At the time it was quite innovative and its location, Merton Abbey Mills, was a new regeneration project in south London. I had not then heard the words "and you must never neglect the oceans or the forests." Part of priesthood has always been the mediation of the

37

glories of the natural world to people. That childlike delight in the intricate and complex wonders of the natural world is essential to being human. It now reaches monumental significance with the advent of global warming and the threats to the future of Earth in the face of political self-deception. A priest is "a man with the child in his eyes". One of the reasons he exists, in the ancient tradition of the shaman, is to alert humanity to the threats to its existence. One of the ways through to that is to delight in all the natural abundance of our planet.

Another understanding of the word 'priest' is to be the ears and eyes of a community. Earlier I suggested that one of the roles of the outsider is perhaps to see clearly what is going on, to try and understand the bigger picture, to piece together the pieces of the human jigsaw. In that sense a priest is always an outsider. Some religious traditions talk about a priest "being set apart". I prefer to think that from time to time out of the depths of my own humanity and my identification with all that is human I have been able to help a few people glimpse beyond the everyday to those things that make us human at our very best. It is, as I said earlier, a question of integrity. Another way of looking at it is the healing of the splits. Almost all of us suffer levels of ambivalence between the ideal that we would love to be and the pragmatism of who we really are. Mark Rylance, the great Shakespearean actor as well as the creator of Thomas Cromwell in the BBC production of *Wolf Hall*, talks about that tension at the heart of every human life. We are all trapped between power and helplessness, pride and shame and order and chaos. It is that ambivalence that we spend our lives seeking to resolve. In this sense a priest is the most human of people because he is the public recognition that those splits exist in all of us, however powerful or powerless we may be.

Integrity is "the dots that really matter". The dots that I had to add up were the reconciliation of my sexual nature to the demands of priesthood. In the end I made the choice to pursue that reconciliation outside of the institutional Church. I fully recognise that there are women and men who manage that conflict and ambivalence within the Church. There have always been women and men in the monastic communities who have celebrated the achievement of holding the two in tension. At one point in my life another Bishop of Southwark, Ronald Bowlby, suggested to me that I had missed my true vocation as a monk. For me the truth is that the passion of sex is too close to the heart of my being for it to be sublimated or ignored. I delight in being a sexual being and I celebrate every fibre of my being that is gay and fulfilled. I could not sublimate it either by leading a hidden, and promiscuous, life or by living a pretend life within an institution that I know does not value me for who I truly am. Some would call that childish innocence. I call it 'the man with the child in his eyes'.

CHAPTER FOUR

WHAT BECOMES OF THE BROKEN HEARTED

"Your vision will become clear only when you look into your own heart...who looks inside, awakes."

(Carl Jung)

I met Tom soon after I moved to Deal in Kent in 2003. Extrovert and a compulsive party animal, Tom was plagued by the knowledge that he was an adopted child. It was also fairly clear that his second marriage was plagued with problems and he had difficulties not only with his stepchildren but also the children of his first marriage. Tom would frequently turn up at my home and Ralph, my partner, and I did all we could to befriend and support him. I spent hours with him and his wife exploring the tensions in their marriage and in separate sessions we explored what it meant to be an adopted child. Through much of that time it felt like dealing with an adolescent boy who had not quite reached adulthood. He plunged from affair to affair never quite able to fulfil his ambivalent sexuality. Then came Valentine's Day 2007. A phone call told me that Tom was dead. He had had a massive stroke. The family contacted me and asked me to take care of all the funeral arrangements. It became clear quite quickly that there was a mixture of resolute Christian faith and healthy agnosticism in his adopted family. What was needed was a funeral that captured some of the ambivalences and was truthful to this complex, and tragic, person.

All my experience at St Martin-in-the-Fields had convinced me that the care of people was at the heart of being a priest. I had also discovered that it is a profoundly human activity. A story like that of Tom's journey provides us with a number of indicators of what I have discovered about compassion and care in the last fifty years. In 1969 I took a year's course at the Richmond Fellowship in London. The emerging Institute was beginning to develop an understanding of how human growth and development is related to the pastoral care of souls. Through a detailed study of the behavioural sciences and psychology I came to understand something of the critical periods of development in human life. But I also gained some understanding of how they can also illuminate some of the moral and spiritual dilemmas that people face. I also caught a first glimpse through an understanding of Carl Jung's work of the significance that ritual, symbols and imagination can play in the care of people.

Through my contacts at the Richmond Fellowship I became involved with a national network of Christian and Jewish carers and counsellors called the Association of Pastoral Care and Counselling (APCC) and for years I was the voluntary National Secretary of that body of people. Today it has been transformed into a section of the British Association of Counselling and Psychotherapy with the subtitle Spirituality. In the 1970s APCC was a pioneering body of people with European and international contacts. The common link was a determination to learn from their humanity and their spirituality. European and international conferences highlighted the cultural and social tensions that influence that kind of exploration. This was focussed for me sharply in 1984 when I led the first workshop on the care of gay people at an international conference in San Francisco. I was bamboozled with every psychological theory about what creates a homosexual person. I also discovered that priests from other parts of the world, and especially Australia, were struggling hard with their sexuality. I also had the rare privilege of meeting a gay imam.

APCC played a vitally important role in the churches of England in the 1970s and 80s. It was the channel through which numerous clergy and lay people were supported in their care of people. Networks of groups in many areas provided a weekly opportunity to explore some of the stress and pain of working in a difficult urban environment. Many clergy worked alone and were often seriously isolated and as a consequence less than effective. The APCC network gave people space and freedom to discuss some of the tougher pastoral situations they faced. Inevitably it was viewed with suspicion by church leaders and there was more than one concerted attempt by conservative churchmen to close it down. It was too resilient for that. Another of its features was the support it provided for women exploring their vocation within the churches. Their contribution to pastoral care and ministry was validated. Years later when the first women were ordained to the Anglican priesthood I sat in Southwark Cathedral looking through the list. Of the 122 women being ordained that day I had been involved in the professional development of seventy-eight of them. It was one of the proudest moments of my life.

In the later stages of my involvement with APCC there was much discussion about its integration with the British Association of Counselling. The disciplines of counselling and psychotherapy had made leaps and bounds in the twentieth century and there was quite rightly a push for good standards of training, supervision and scrutiny. During the 1980s those professional standards were being developed especially after exposure of some of the pastoral craziness in the west of the USA. APCC became a division of the British Association of Counselling and continues today in its transformed role.

That was the framework within which I derived 'a filing cabinet' of insights and skills about the care people need not least at the junctures of crisis in their lives. What is the heart of that endeavour? I believe it is about creating Hope. What most people in crisis really need is the sense that this will not go on forever, that there is hope that a different future is possible. The willingness to share their pain and enter as skilfully as possible into the heart of their dilemma is to offer the possibility of hope. Tom had placed much of his hope on a new family and the discovery of real parents. But both were proving elusive. The new family was erupting into periodic violence and the 'real' mother did not want to know. His 'real father' had died long before this time. They were, if you like, self-delusions. Tom was pursuing false hopes.

Working with Tom I tried to help towards the insight that his hope lay in the discovery of his self-worth, a worth not dependent on distant mothers or absent fathers but on the recognition of his own intrinsic worth as a human being. What I did not know at the time, but discovered during his funeral, was that he was highly regarded by his work colleagues and they placed inestimable worth on his contribution as a team manager. The delivery of Hope is a profound spiritual concept perhaps because it is one of the rocks on which the human endeavour stands. A future of hope certainly lies at the centre of all the great religious traditions. And like all great traditions it is capable of distortion. Many Christian sects have grown up around the idea that a community is living in the last days. The group called ISIS in the Muslim community has a conviction that its centre, a town on the Iraq-Syria border, is the place of the final showdown between good and evil. Perhaps that explains the attraction of young people to its pernicious community. These millenarian movements have always led to false hope and often tragic outcomes. They are the embodiment of false Hope.

Pastoral care at its best is about the realisation of hope based on a true understanding of the human endeavour and a realistic grasp of all the human dislocations that have caused the pain. Lots of people live in exile from the people they are meant to be. Tom had so many fantasies about family life he never really embraced his adopted family. He idealised them to such a degree that he could not connect with them in a healthy way. The same applied to his other adopted family, the woman and stepchildren of the second marriage. In his frustration at their being less than his ideal he erupted with violence. I, too, was well aware that I was the idealised 'good father' who would make everything right. The empathy required to enter into this world of self-deception is often costly. More than once I was phoned by the police in the early hours of the morning: "It's your choice. Either take him to your home or we will lock him up in a cell for the night." Pastoral care and pastoral choices are not for the faint-hearted.

Tom also helps us understand the way in which personal pain can be a symptom of a malfunction in either a larger family or a bigger community. His idealism about families derived to some extent from the myths that were promulgated in both his adopted families. The self-image of himself as an extrovert party animal was fed by the community in which he lived. There were myths in the first adopted family about what really constitutes a Christian family and the huge emotional investment placed in those myths. Years before I ever met Tom I was preaching a sermon at St Mary the Boltons about the 'Family'. It was based on the Scripture readings for the day. The Christian scriptures are highly ambivalent about what is meant by family and it is certainly not the nuclear family we embrace today. Halfway through the sermon a large hymn book came hurtling towards the pulpit and hit me between the eyes! What is really interesting is who it was thrown by. Several months earlier I had had extensive discussions with a couple about their wish to remarry. Each had had previous marriages and in the case of the woman, three divorces. Because they were regular members of the congregation I had agreed, after much discussion and soul searching to conduct a new marriage. Their gratitude came in the form of a flying hymn book. I had dared question the sacred cow of the family!

Tom suffered from the myths that were embedded in the family story. He also suffered from the myths about what creates a good life in the community in which he lived. His violence was frequently fuelled by excessive alcohol dependence. Part of the small-town fantasy was driven by a social conviction that drinking a lot was crucial to having a good time. In Tom's case it contributed to his early death. He was not the only male to go that way in the small town where he lived. Again his personal myth was being fed by a broader social phenomenon. He needed to drink to keep up the persona of the heterosexual adult male although much of his behaviour was akin to the adolescent male. Again it was self-deception. This is probably one of the major advances in psychological insights and practice from the earlier years of the twentieth century. Social and cultural norms within community feed the myths that people live by often at an unconscious level. Understanding those myths is a key to assisting and helping people through emotional and mental pain. For that reason carers and counsellors... and priests and ministers... need to be embedded in their communities.

Tom never fulfilled his human destiny and it was my responsibility to create his funeral and offer pastoral care to his family, friends and community. In 1986 I had written *Only Connect*, a study of worship, liturgy and ritual from the perspective of pastoral care. The book starts with a quotation from Gerald Manley Hopkins:

"Since, tho' he is under the world's splendour and wonder,

His mystery must be instressed, stressed;

For I greet him the days I meet him,

And bless when I understand." (*The Wreck of the Deutschland*)

That book explored the psychological insights about ritual and symbols and how they related to the care of human beings. Since my retirement from the Church of England I have been asked numerous times to create events that would celebrate the life of individuals whilst enabling a community to mourn and grieve. Frequently I am asked if those events can be free of religious language and symbols. It is not necessarily the case that people are antagonistic to spiritual insight but they do not want the dead person's integrity compromised. In Tom's case I constructed a Christian funeral service for the family and later a celebration free of religious language in a pub garden. The final act was to scatter his ashes on the waves close to his beloved cycle path.

Rituals, like funerals, are essential for human health. They are of paramount importance in enabling whole communities to handle tragic events. After the Hillsborough disaster a community ritual had to be created to contain the enormity of the grief being experienced. But that containment is also a way of enabling a community to move on, to pass beyond the tragic to a future of Hope. One of the really disabling features of human life is the holding on to grief and the past. It paralyses both individuals and communities. It can at best cause an unhealthy nostalgia for the past. At worst it creates a morbid grief reaction with emotional and sometimes physical consequences. The town where I live suffered an IRA bombing and occasionally I feel the town is held back by an unhealthy nostalgia for that time and that event. Hope is not about indulging the past. It is about embracing the future with all the lessons learnt from that past. In a second book I wrote, *A Step Too Far*, I concluded:

"Reconciliation demands that someone steps out beyond the normal boundaries of human life: it invites a person, a group or a nation to walk beyond the established frontiers so that something new can happen... It is the only way that change can happen and peace be established."

When that book was published the English reviews were lukewarm. The ones from Ireland were rave reviews. I knew that I had touched on something deeply important.

I have written at length about pastoral care because it has been central to my life and to an understanding of who I am. I have endeavoured from time to time to tame my natural instincts by learning more skills and focussing on those changes in our culture and society that shape how people think about themselves. I have always understood myself in relation to other people and by sharing their pain with me other people have enriched my life beyond any measurement. That experience has also deepened my understanding of priesthood so that it belongs more to the altar of the world than to the altar of the church. It is possible to exercise a secular priesthood and that is what I have endeavoured to be in the years since I resigned from any formal engagement with the Church of England. I do not need the institutional church to define who I am. I do need humanity and compassion and care to challenge me about who I might be. Again I end this chapter with those compelling words of Kate Gross:

"The dots that really matter aren't the ones you decide you want to do, but how you want to be."

Or as Oscar Wilde put it:

"Only Connect"

CHAPTER FIVE

FIELDS OF GOLD

*"...one day people will touch and talk, perhaps,
easily..."*

(A. S. J Tessimond)

Here are two stories. When I worked for the Anglican Church's mission and aid agency, USPG, I was responsible for the Indian Ocean region. I had been sent to a regional consultation and specifically to investigate an aid project, a pig-breeding farm, in the south-east of Madagascar. I arrived in Tamatave on the east coast and was told we would set out the next day. We would be travelling in a four-by-four, then by boat and then by foot to reach this remote area. When the four-by-four reached the river crossing I was told "Ah no boats... we return to Tamatave." I questioned the local bishop at length about the aid project and received no coherent answers. We then left for the consultation in Mauritius. For three days I persisted with my questioning about the project until the bishop's son-in-law cracked: "*Ah, mon ami*," he said, "*c'est un reve dans le ciel!*" (It's a dream in the sky.) I persisted. He cracked again: his father in law, the bishop, was building his retirement palace with the aid money.

The second story. During the time that I sat on the General Synod of the Church of England I was also acting as the voluntary secretary of the World Development Movement, a secular agency that had been set up to campaign at national government level for an increase in the national Aid budget to developing countries but also to move the whole issue of Aid away from the notion of charity towards development goals for developing countries affected by poverty, disease and malnutrition. In the mid-1980s members of the British government were questioning the aid target of 0.7% of GNP and it was seriously under threat. In the General Synod I challenged the then Archbishop of Canterbury, Robert Runcie, to confront the Prime Minister, Margaret Thatcher, about this weakening of resolve. He made a lukewarm response to my challenge. When the debate was over I went to see him and challenged him again. A few days later he paid a visit to Downing Street and within months the 0.7% target was restored as official government policy.

I have always been fascinated by politics and by what political leadership means. These two stories, from the same period of my life, highlight the complexities and ambiguities that can be involved in political process. Overseas aid focuses very clearly how international economics can so easily become prey to political corruption even in institutions like the Anglican Church. There is an irony in the fact that I was managing the transfer of aid to Madagascar whilst at the same time questioning the whole process of giving aid by my engagement with the World Development Movement. But politics is messy and often conflicting goals have to be held in tension. It's not for nothing that it is known as the art of the possible. Disengagement with politics, especially national politics, has characterised the second half of my lifetime. Political leadership has lost its roots in the mesh of everyday life and is rightly called into question by anarchic comedians like Russell Brand. But politics is the framework for an evolving democracy and is fundamental for the management of economics in a globalised world.

My engagement with national government taught me a fundamental lesson about any form of community leadership, in or out of the church. Research is essential not just in marshalling the facts but also in engaging with the bigger picture. I said in an earlier chapter that the truth is often found in Appendix 4 of a document. Politics is also the art of the artful and politicians are past masters at creating complexity and obscurity. I was to learn this again when I left the institutional church and launched into a second career. My partner, Ralph, had left a career in the retail restaurant business and was unemployed. We happened upon a regeneration site in south-west London. It had been the old Liberty factory site and was being regenerated as a collection of shops, restaurants and a weekend market known as Merton Abbey Mills. For the next ten years it was a thriving and chaotic location for all kinds of entrepreneurial activity. It was where Ralph and I established Greencades, a shop specialising in herbs and spices, aromatherapy and other natural products. It became the biggest shop in the complex and for ten years the business grew until we were employing ten full- and part-time staff. We were importing goods from developing countries so I felt a strange continuity with my past, especially when the cloves from Tamatave arrived! For most of those ten years I was elected as the Chair of the residents' association and my political skills were further honed by negotiations with the management team.

However by the dawn of the new millennium it was obvious that there were serious threats to the regenerated site. A large area of brownfield land had served as a car park for the thousands of visitors to the site every weekend. Sainsburys had abandoned their obligation under a planning agreement to build a swimming pool for the borough of Merton on it. It was prime development land. And so began my engagement with town and country planning. After a number of false starts a company called Countryside Properties showed an interest and it was clear that the car park which was essential in an area of meagre public transport was under threat. Much of what was proposed was alien to the ethos and character of the regeneration site. It was also a historic archaeological site. Merton Abbey was where Thomas Becket had been educated. Three medieval kings and queens had been crowned there. The Liberty site had earlier housed some of the Huguenots who brought lavender- and rose-growing to south London. Later William Morris had established his textile works nearby. Layer upon layer of historic events gave the site a very special significance.

The developers had a different vision. Burger King and Virgin Active, Premier Inn and 370 multi-storey flats. Initially we were able to persuade the local planning authority that the proposed plans were alien to the historic buildings that formed the Merton Abbey site. There was serious incongruity between the different elevations and the destruction of the car park would damage the long-term commercial interests of the businesses on the regeneration site. We won the first battle. But at this point we had to face the complexity of the planning process in London. The Mayor of London had become part of the process and it was not long before he was accepting a contribution of 3.7 million from the developer in return for agreeing to no affordable housing on the site! The 3.7 million was to be given to the Borough of Merton to build affordable housing elsewhere! The local councillors admitted that they had no idea where the land existed for that building programme. In addition to this Transport of London insisted that there was no need for car parking because it was a policy to encourage all visits by bicycle and public transport. I invited Ken Livingstone, the Mayor, to come on his bike and we would provide him with a large ceramic flowerpot, a small carpet and a number of other items to take home on his bike! I never heard from him again!

We fought on but lost the next two battles... and the war. Today Merton Abbey Mills has lost most of its energy, is dwarfed by some of the ugliest buildings in south London and numerous employment opportunities were lost. Any hope of retaining some of the vital historic references that give a community its roots has been lost. A golden opportunity for the Museum of London to create a satellite museum celebrating this multi-layered heritage hit the buffers early on. It is a classic example of the kind of development that is defacing the face of England. In 2003 Ralph and I saw that the future of our business was at risk. We told the staff that we were thinking of relocating and helped them all find other employment. By the end of 2003 we had relocated our business to the town of Deal on the east Kent coast.

I had not been in Deal for more than a year when I received a telephone call: "I remember you. You were that guy that fought to save Merton Abbey Mills in south London. How about taking up the planning brief for the Deal Society?" The die was cast. The local authority was about to launch a consultation on a twenty-year plan and there were fears that some aspects of the plan could be a major threat to the historic character of the town. I couldn't resist. I had become fascinated by the part that planning plays in shaping places. I had seen it destroy the historic character of part of south London so I knew the threats as well as the opportunities that can be created by politicians who often fail to grasp the long term vision in favour of short term economic gain. I also knew full well that historic heritage and conservation areas could be put at risk by politicians meeting short term targets especially in relation to strategic housing targets. It was not long before I was elected the Chairman of the Deal Society and co-opted onto the town council planning committee.

Every one of us develops different selves over the course of our lives. We try on different selves for different situations, different relationship, and different places. A narrative will run through the whole threading together the different parts of the story. I had gone from priest to entrepreneur to local community leader but through it all was the conviction that I could make a difference however small that might be. Planning is about making a difference because at all kinds of levels it changes the character of a place, it reshapes environments and it can transform the mediocre into something that enhances and enriches a community.

That is also why collaboration and community engagement must be at the heart of the town planning process. Despite feeble attempts by national government ministers to introduce neighbourhood plans and other forms of Localism the reality is that the balance of power still rests with planning officers. Together with that the power of locally elected politicians is curtailed especially in local authorities where cabinet government operates. That is made even worse by the absurd party political battles that are fought when what is needed is a high degree of collaboration in local development. Most party politics are largely irrelevant at a really local level. Engaging local people in the decisions that directly affect the quality of their everyday lives should be at the heart of the political process. Planning does affect how long you wait for a doctor's appointment, whether your child has a place in a local primary school or whether there are enough dentists to go round in an area of increased housing.

Sustainable development can only be achieved by democratic means. Griff Rhys Jones, the comedian and President of Civic Voice, has said:

"It is time to change the ways things are done and to bring communities genuinely to the heart of planning and place making."

National and local governments both have the obvious desire to control things centrally. Local shops and offices are frequently owned by multinational companies. The result is that local people feel powerless to effect what happens in their locality. That can deepen a sense of alienation and at worst develop an environment in which all forms of antisocial behaviour breed. There is vast scope for improving the public realm in many of our cities, towns and villages and a lot of that does not require the planning system. In Deal the renovation of a small theatre has brought incalculable benefits to the community's life. When people are engaged in shaping what is important for them, people begin to own that place and to put value on its future development. There needs to be an adult debate about the future of local government and how local people can be empowered to shape the communities in which they live. Economic growth, public health, crime reduction and social and racial cohesion are all dependent on achieving that level of community engagement.

Planning is also about developing the big picture. One of the threads running through my own narrative is the two tiny words 'only connect'. Connecting up the dots in a local community is a vital element in community leadership. This applies especially in the realm of housing. Building enough homes has become one of the political obsessions of the early twenty-first century. Clearly there is a crisis largely because of the failure of successive governments to create sufficient social housing. But the baby boom generation of the post-War period has also spread the myth that house ownership is central to human happiness. The result is that significant tracts of England have been covered with housing estates of such mediocrity that future generations will despair of the lack of vision. Most imaginative architectural planning has been put into large scale public building projects. The result is that domestic architecture has been left to second and third rate architects and planners. The green fields that have become pots of gold to property developers have been paved over by construction companies creating estates lacking community focus and often a lamentable lack of social and cultural infrastructure. Short-sighted commercial gain has taken the place of finding the bigger picture. One of the strategic priorities for housing growth is to match it with those places where there is vigorous economic growth. The Centre for Cities has named ten places in England where the need for new housing is being created by economic acceleration in the immediate area. Political mantras about endless house building everywhere need to be replaced by much more focussed planning. There also needs to be an act of political courage. It may be the case that a property-owning democracy is not the future shape of the country. We may need to adopt a much more European model where renting property becomes a more widespread social norm. It goes against the grain of every idol that Britain has developed in my lifetime. It may be economic reality. It would certainly involve a revolution in local government thinking about the priority of social housing. It would also involve radical change in the ways that national house builders think because they will do everything in their power to dodge any social dimension to their planning.

I wrote earlier that perhaps I prefer being a small fish in a big pond rather than a big fish in a small pond. Nowhere has that been truer than my time in the town of Deal. I had the apparent disadvantage of being the outsider and a marginal person. But by becoming embedded in the community, listening to its concerns, researching with care the strategic developments about its future I hope I have turned an obvious disadvantage to a community advantage. I have followed that charge "not to neglect the oceans and the forests" and tried to fight for the protection of the fields of gold. As with other areas of England, some of our green and golden fields are being grabbed by politicians for their high growth vanity projects. Generations to come will regret the sprawling housing estates that are being built on the edges of the town. But over against that the historic centre and the multiple levels of heritage are being protected. It is part of a secular priesthood to protect the fields of gold, to ensure that future generations inherit a place shaped by centuries of confused development, a place fit for purpose for healthy and vibrant life.

CHAPTER SIX

SHOPPING

"The real story behind our current fight for the High Street is about people. ... Their dedication has made the place they live, work, socialise and shop a place they can cherish and be proud of."

(Mary Portas)

When I resigned from the Church in 1990 and announced that I was setting up a small business with my partner, Ralph, I received many anxious and angry challenges. It was as if I was off to dance with the Devil. Twenty-five years later it is perhaps easier to understand those reactions than it was then. The banking crisis of 2008 laid bare the ways in which big business had undermined the fabric of society, increased social inequality and nearly brought the world to the brink of economic collapse. Many of the assumptions that were hidden in 1990 were exposed in their human horror nearly twenty years later. The revolving door between the political classes and big business has been laid bare. The ability of large companies to lobby government is now much more understood. We even understand how major accountants can take consultancies in the Treasury in order to frame laws that can then be circumvented. It strikes me as ironic that the door to number 11 Downing Street is a solid wooden door. In reality it is one of the fastest moving revolving doors in history.

The creation of wealth by the small business community is a world away from all this. In fact small business is the lifeblood of the British community and a generator of jobs and economic vitality in thousands of local communities. It is also a community of innovation and creativity. During the twenty-five years that we ran our small business we encountered dozens of entrepreneurs driving forward new and imaginative ways of doing business. We saw the quality of British design advance and accelerate. Britain found its way out of post-Second World War austerity into a vibrant and world-beating creative community.

This was partly driven by a fundamental change in the nature of shopping. In the latter part of the twentieth century shopping had ceased to be solely a functional activity and had become part of the leisure industry. We opened our business in the new complex of Merton Abbey Mills in south-west London. The site that had once been the home of the innovative company Liberty was transformed into a complex of shops, hospitality venues and a vast weekend market devoted to arts and crafts. It was visited by thousands of people and in the period before Sunday trading was introduced it was one of the main sources of retail activity in that part of London. The market created a space for all kinds of small entrepreneurs to develop their business ideas and we were among them. It was a boiling pot of new ideas and the punters loved it. A small theatre and regular concerts of live music added to its vitality bringing together artists, musicians and people on the cutting edge of new drama and dramatic innovation. Although we did not know it at the time it was probably a small vision of what the British High Street would need to become if it was to survive.

In his book *The Road to Little Dribbling* Bill Bryson revisits many of the places across Britain that he had visited twenty years before when he wrote *Notes from a Small Island*. In the new book he returns to one theme again and again. The demise and changes that have happened in the British High Street. It is an interesting observation because he makes it clear that like many men he is not that fond of shopping! He observes the loss of small utility businesses... the ironmonger, the butcher, the bakery, the greengrocer. Much of that has been replaced with cafes, wine bars and shops selling planks of wood with pious sayings! The reasons for those changes are well researched. The inability of successive governments to resist the astronomical growth of out-of-town shopping centres was the first major death blow. This has been further accelerated by the explosion in Internet shopping. Those two social revolutions have devastated conventional shopping in many traditional high streets.

At the beginning of the twenty-first century national government recognised that this social revolution was reaching a critical level. They appointed Mary Portas, a business guru, to produce a report on what was ailing the High Street. Among a whole set of proposals aimed at reforming business rates and stimulating new innovations Ms Portas proposed the creation of a group of Portas Pilots, a number of towns that would receive a large injection of cash to promote new initiatives in the evolution of high street communities. Towns, cities and villages were invited to submit their proposals and initially twelve would be selected. I was asked to chair the group that would make the proposal for my new home town of Deal. We had established our business in the town after leaving London and the devastation of our business community in south-west London by unscrupulous property developers. The local chamber of trade had made a ludicrous first attempt at the bid for Portas funding, a proposal that became a laughing stock among many of the local retail community. So as the Biblical phrase goes "the lot fell on me".

The group was composed of local retailers, councillors and technology entrepreneurs. It did not take me long to recognise that where government funding is available local councillors are lurking like hawks ready to pounce! The group was paralysed initially by that presence and standing up to that petty civic power absorbed lots of energy. Nevertheless a bid was put together and submitted hours before the deadline. We never became one of the Portas Pilots and I was relieved that that was the case. We did qualify for a smaller grant and that was to fund some useful initiatives on Deal High Street in the years following. A Town Team was formed and for a time it provided a focus for new thinking and some initiatives. And then out of the blue a national paper, the *Daily Telegraph*, named Deal High Street of the Year. I suspect that that did more good than any amount of national government funding.

That experience has given me some new perspectives on the whole business of shopping. Deal is an extremely fortunate place. We have many of the elements that make for a vibrant local economy. Our supermarkets are within walking distance of the town centre. No out-of-town centres suck life out of the town centre. The high street has a great balance of small independent stores and national chains which help to anchor the retail community. There is a large creative community of artists and musicians. On a Saturday morning the pedestrian precinct might be electrified by a large group of dancers breaking into a routine. The town centre still had butchers, fishmongers, bakers and an ironmonger. There are over thirty venues where you can find a half-decent cup of coffee and only one of them is a national chain. There are three markets all run by the local town council. All those elements together create a chemistry that keeps a high street vibrant. That is not to say that there are not risks. One of the great ironies is this. At the same time that Deal was declared High Street of the Year we announced that our business was closing after twenty-five years. It was a bitter pill to swallow. But we were exhausted by trying to fight not just avaricious councillors but also the almighty power of the Internet.

What have I learnt about the character of Britain, and indeed the character of myself, by this engagement with shopping? First of all there is a radical difference between big and small business. During the Portas Pilot episode I attempted to get letters of endorsement for the bid. Small businesses produced their version within hours. With Marks and Spencer the local manager had to take it through endless levels of management to agree a one-line endorsement. It took nearly a month to agree a one-line letter. But of course it is the hidden agenda that really exerts the power. Marks and Spencer did not like Mary Portas! This atrophy in big business devours creative energy and sucks away at the human spirit. It must have a stultifying effect on business at many levels. In contrast the multi-skilled small entrepreneur enjoys a freedom that releases energy for innovation and imaginative engagement with customers.

The Portas Pilot exercise has not been a major national success story. Some of the areas receiving the 100K grants have found it very difficult to find ways to use the funds. In other cases the money has been frittered away on ludicrous projects. But I suspect that one of the major obstacles lies within the retail business community itself. It was almost impossible to achieve any serious co-operation. The national chains on the whole distanced themselves from the whole enterprise and refused to engage largely through the complex inertia I described earlier. Many small businesses are caught up in the business of survival that they have little energy left for co-operative projects. Like a lot of civic service, businesses were only too happy to let a few "mugs" get on with it. It was never actively opposed or supported. If it happened it happened. If it did not it did not and frankly nobody much cared. National government ministers danced down to the town once we were named High Street of the Year hoping to discover some magical formula that would save the British High Street. As in most of life, the truth is that no magic exists. Some places are luckier than others in their historical development, in the combination of personalities at a given time, in the willingness of people to sacrifice some of their own freedom to nurture the greater good by standing up to some of the petty little tin gods who run the local political powerhouse.

Shopping has also taught me more about the human personality. In the television series *Little Britain* David

Walliams plays a character that turns up in shops looking for the most obscure item imaginable. He typifies a character that most shopkeepers will be more than familiar with. It is the loner who seeks social engagement through power play and challenge. He also pushes the shopkeeper to the very limit of patience and tolerance. His question is: "Can I break down the professional boundary of this individual?" Just occasionally he or she can be the ally of the shoplifter; the one who distracts and confuses whilst another takes items for the heroin addict's shopping list. It is a masterly portrait of shopping at its most impotent and futile.

As shopping has developed more and more as a leisure pursuit it seems to have heightened the difference gender plays in the shopping experience. Women and men shop differently. For many women shopping is now their major leisure pursuit. They are happy to spend endless hours simply looking around shops, however big or small, however fascinating or excruciatingly boring. They often need nothing. They can be past mistresses at returning what they bought an hour earlier. They will spend five minutes searching in their purses for just the right money. Many women have all the time in the world, for shopping! Men on the other hand appear to be much more focussed but also much more cynical about the whole experience. If a man is buying a greetings card you can be sure he will almost always have the right money ready to pay. But he will always be the first to try for the discount or the deal. He can have a sense of triumph when he finds what he wants. I remember one famous weather forecaster being triumphant about finding a sun fridge magnet. And an equally famous newscaster who was over the moon about finding a 5p wooden lavender ball for his wife's Christmas present.

Shopping is not always confined to shopping. A shop can be a community centre. It can also be a confessional. I was deeply shocked on the two occasions we closed the business, first in London and then in Deal, at the range of human emotion it evoked. We had people shouting at us in rage. We had people weeping on our shoulders. Shops sometimes carry more meaning than the actual things they sell. That is partly because you, as the shopkeeper, are vulnerable and easily accessible. I have had more people pour out their pain and troubled psyches in a shop than I ever had at confessional times as a priest. It was once said of our shop that it appealed to all of the human senses. That may be one of the clues why people felt comfortable in it. Because they felt comfortable they felt more at ease with themselves. I am not saying that shops are confessionals! But they often serve more purposes than just plain shopping. The David Walliams character is a profoundly lonely man.

It was a profound change moving from being a priest to being a shopkeeper. But I never felt diminished by that change. I also feel that I have contributed to the sum total of human happiness as much by one as the other. I do not even feel that one was the betrayal of the other. I have exercised as much civic leadership as I ever did as a priest. I have nurtured and encouraged human talent in the wonderful staff we have employed over the years. I have quietly counselled and comforted simply because of my availability. Lots of churches could do well to think of the high-street shop as a model for their being in the community. I hope by the quality of our service and the vibrancy of our products we enriched some people's lives. Shopping certainly extended my experience of being human.

CHAPTER SEVEN

I WILL SURVIVE

"...a man looks in a mirror to see his face, and at art to see his soul. But modern man has no soul to see."

(Paul Murray: *The Mark and the Void*)

Gargantua might well be the fictional name for the political universe that we live in at the beginning of the twenty-first century. When I contrast the first twenty years of my life with the fifty that followed it is the scale of the human endeavour that really strikes me. The warning was there early on. I have never forgotten that my life as a very small child was under the clouds of Hiroshima and Nagasaki. That massive escalation of war and the dark clouds that spread through the human psyche were to infect our understanding of the world and the meaning of what it is to be human today. It was as if the shadow at the heart of human personality had taken control and released the forces of Hell upon the earth.

Size matters. It matters very much when we begin to contemplate the conditions within which people thrive and find a sense of place in the world. I grew up in a small town but spent most of my working life in big cities. I now live in a small town again. I know that both have vulnerabilities and strengths and neither is a truly comfortable place within which to fulfil all the aspirations of living. But that is compounded by the forces of globalisation and the escalation of growth in almost every aspect of the world that impacts on our everyday existence.

It is often said of a business that it is "too big to fail". That inability to fail develops from the complexity of the relationship between big business and the political system, whether that is local and national government, pan-European institutions, the international bodies of sport like FIFA or the mega lobbying industry. The new Establishment that has developed over the course of my lifetime is one in which the socio-political-economic complex has become the driving force of human endeavour, or perhaps I should say inhuman endeavour. The political and business classes have jumped into bed together faster than two gay men after a drunken night in a gay bar! In the 1950s and early 1960s it felt as if scandals had at least a human face. Whether it was the Profumo affair or the 'gay' scandals involving politicians and patricians there was a human scale both to the offences and to the damage that they caused. Today the scale of the scandals is hidden behind not just a smokescreen of spin but also a 'Berlin Wall' of political co-operation between the media, politicians and big business. Whereas the Establishment used to be an insidious "old boys' network" (and it was, with a few remarkable exceptions, the boys) today it is a multi-layered, multinational, pan-global complex that is virtually out of control.

The gargantuan state is not simply restricted to the Establishment; it penetrates almost every aspect of living. The food industry's scandalous treatment of animals and the resultant abuses of human health are another example of where size matters. The regularity with which food scandals occur are largely the result of big business driving prices down and the inhuman care of animals up. The supermarkets are a brilliant example of "business too big to fail". But, of course, they do and they are. It is no coincidence that the Big Four are now selling off vast tracts of land that they land banked for expansion and are experimenting with stores that are smaller, more local and in some cases more responsive to local suppliers. Jamie Oliver has recently challenged the British government about its inability to deal with the levels of sugar in children's drinks. He has also exposed the ways in which the drinks industry not only has a massive lobbying industry influencing the decisions of civil servants and government ministers, but also the inability of regulatory bodies to label products accurately.

Food and health are intimately related and the connection between the two is one of the great social advances of the twentieth century. When I was growing up in rural Suffolk virtually nobody saw the connexions between obesity and the mental and physical health of people. That applied equally to issues like smoking cigarettes and the excessive intake of alcohol. One of the biggest secrets on the housing estate where I grew up was the police inspector's abuse of his wife and children through his abuse of alcohol. And the Inspector of Public Health lived next door to us! The National Health

71

Service is one of the greatest creations of my lifetime. By that I mean the availability of free health care at the point of need. I do not mean the gargantuan institution that is now virtually beyond human control. The importance of the NHS in the national psyche can never be under estimated. If Britain has a local or regional god it is the NHS. Obeisance is paid to it by politicians of every single hue and it is the constant subject of political and economic debate. It is almost literally the elephant in the room. The institutions providing the nation's health care have grown beyond a scale where human well-being can be nurtured. That is not to denigrate the heroes who keep the vast machines running: they too are being dehumanised by the vastness of Gargantua.

Scandals involving the care of children almost without exception reveal the complexity of agencies and institutions involved in their care. It is not unknown for up to a dozen agencies being involved in the support of the family. The cry from the family is often, "there was nobody on our side". Review after review proposes better levels of cooperation and communication and partnership... and then the next horror movie of abuse and torture and pornographic degradation emerges in the media. The words of a thousand pious reports are revealed as just that. Words. Words. Words. The education system is part of that institutional complexity. It too had grown beyond a truly human scale. But that is compounded especially in the early years by national tests and imposed curricula that alienate the teachers let alone the children. Schools have become places of rote learning rather than oases of creative endeavour. Later on the so-called pursuit of academic excellence alienates vast numbers of children who need to develop innate skills and talents that are crucial for the health of the national economy. Education has become monochromatic and in that sense it abuses natural human talent.

Four national house builders dominate the housing industry in Britain. At the last count they owned over 300,000 building plots between them. On the other hand politicians say that we need 200,000 new homes a year. There is something radically wrong with the creation of homes fit to live in. The four major house builders are all pumping out factory housing, that is large housing estates often with houses that lack appropriate human scale. Some of the rooms are hardly big enough for a large dog to be comfortable in. But that endeavour has also been severely curtailed not, as many politicians claim, by over complicated planning laws but rather by the lack of human skills and building materials resulting from the 2008 global crisis. Two of the factors holding back the creation of homes are the lack of bricks and the lack of bricklayers! Both were devastated partly by that crisis and partly by the political inertia at national and local government. In contrast to this both in other parts of Europe and in the USA building authorities and developers have been releasing small plots of land where architects, prospective home owners and builders work together to create homes. In the historical studies I have done about the town I live in, Deal in Kent, it has become apparent that this is how the town evolved in the first part of the nineteenth century. Small plots were sold off to meet population growth and housing need in the town. This is in marked contrast to the vast housing estates now being built on the edges of the town with no population growth or economic justification other than a High Growth Strategy developed by the local authority. A strategy that took no account of all the issues raised by local people about the human and physical infrastructure needed to sustain that level of house building. Gargantua and the Establishment win again!

Steve Hilton in his radical and breathtaking book *More Human* has argued that this emergence of a socio-political-economic complex on this gargantuan scale is in fact diminishing not just the meaning of being human but the very essences that make human life truly fulfilling. In his critical analysis of the forces that have created institutions beyond a human scale he makes a plea for human beings and their vital mental, emotional and physical needs to be put again at the focus of all political endeavours. People need to be put back in control of the institutions that make the framework for living at all stages of life. During the course of the book he cites numerous examples of innovative ideas and practical projects where people in housing and education, in the food industry and national health schemes are advancing a different kind of future. Technology is playing a critical role in that explosion of new thinking and creative action. Technology is a two-edged sword but, applied to the task of making life more human, it creates powers for good.

At the heart of the Christian faith that I have lived in and out of most of my life there is a fundamental idea without which not a lot of it makes much sense. It is the belief that the human has been given ultimate and lasting value. In simple terms Jesus is what human life is all about. That does not mean that the pious and the virtuous and the moral and the good have all been validated. It means that being human in all its glorious aspiration and in all its pornographic degradation has been given value. The deepest darknesses of human nature are capable of transformation into melodies of the most sublime music.

The Christian churches have never been comfortable with this complexity and that is perhaps why I could not survive within one of them. I felt my complex humanity was being throttled to death. I guess that is why millions of people today give the churches little time. They don't feel that their humanity is safe in any church's hands.

Yet in the face of Gargantua it is precisely the human that we need to reassert. We need, as Steve Hilton argues, to celebrate how we add value to the business of being human. Being inhuman is not part of the natural order of things. A world that is too big and impersonal and distant is not how it needs to be. People not being in control of their lives are not the cultural and religious inheritance of the British people. Anonymous and industrialised machines delivering food, health care, education and housing need not be the everyday norms. We know that we are happiest when we relate to one another in small scale and intimate ways. When life is organised on a human scale we relax, discover our better nature and start to affirm and value others whatever their cultural or social background. Gargantua creates social anxiety. It alienates and belittles. Social policy needs to defy that and bring people much closer to structures and organisations that enhance rather than diminish life. There are parts of our human family that are deeply undervalued: children and very old people. We need to give them back their humanity and insure that the institutions they live and breathe in affirm that humanity.

So we start with people. Everyone wants to say... at least in the depths of their psyche, "I will survive". We need to put how humans learn, how they feel, what they need right back at the heart of our political action and our principles and values for living. That requires empathy, ability to feel and experience the world as others do. That is in remarkably short supply in the Age of the Selfie. One of the devastating effects of a world called Gargantua is that it blunts self-awareness and nurtures self-absorption. Big Value means what works for me not what is in the interest of a healthy society. Gargantua at its most brutal is thousands of people fleeing from their homeland and beginning an exodus that the world has not seen for generations. It is too simplistic to say, "Oh we should take them into our own homes". We need to begin by understanding the cultural, social and religious ideals that separate us. Then we could begin to perceive the common links in our humanity. The refugee crises of the early twenty-first century have exposed the brutal limits of a world based on gargantuan thinking. The politico-military complex of the Establishment has created the conditions within which those crises happen. Empathy might at least be the beginning of a better world. As would diplomatic and political resolutions of the wars from which the people flee.

Another clue to making life and our communities more human is to stress again and again that the local matters. Localism has become a kind of passive political speak. But its essence is at the heart of human survival. Political institutions and local government need to be really local so that people feel they have a say in what is happening within their community. The 1974 Local Government Act created structures that are too far removed from where people feel things matter. Deal is only eight miles from Dover and yet most people feel the headquarters of their local authority might as well be at the other end of Kent. It is not for nothing that they call the local authority headquarters Mount Whitfield; a remote hill miles from what really concerns them in their lives. Local politicians get sucked in to Gargantua. They are often very bad at communicating the concerns of their constituents and engaging citizens in the issues that will affect their lives. As at all levels of government many of the local politicians have become career politicians, sadly often more concerned with their self-aggrandisement.

I have often been called a maverick, someone who refuses to fit in. That was certainly why I could not survive in the Established Church of English. But mavericks are essential to the health of a good society. Historically it was the Fool who exposed the foibles of the Court establishment. Another way of looking at it is someone who is ready to spill the beans. It is one of the strengths of being gay. Gay people in the end "come out"; they spill the beans about themselves. That is a fine training for playing a part in civic life. Whereas confidentiality is a critical part of protecting human life, it can also be the means by which the Establishment keeps power in its own hands. It is a way of protecting the status quo. It is also the way in which the Establishment ensures that power stays where it is. Communities need mavericks; they need people to ensure that others have the ability to get to grips with those things that undermine real local community. The maverick, the Fool, is always well armed. They have researched and briefed themselves; they know what the policies and issues are; they have dug deep and know that it will be Appendix 4 that will reveal the real truth of what is going on. They will usually spot the innovators, those with ideas that can bring breakthroughs and new life. You will rarely hear them say, "Oh, we tried that before and it never worked".

There is a very disconcerting end to the Steve Hilton book. Like the war poster "Your country needs you" Hilton points straight at the reader and says: if you want life to be more human then it is down to you. Britain, the world, needs more independently minded people who are prepared to engage in civic service for the overall good of their communities. At many levels of local government party politics is dead in the water. It is totally irrelevant. Instead local communities need independent people with creative and imaginative ideas who really care about the future of that community. They do not need to be great thinkers but they do need great resilience. Nobody should underestimate the entrenched power of Gargantua. Above all they need one another so that mutual support and value become the norms not the exceptions. I will always be an outsider but I believe passionately in teams being that. The risks are very great. Our survival is at stake. Go on singing Gloria Gaynor, we need to hear the anthem: "I will survive".

CHAPTER EIGHT

HANDBAGS AND GLADRAGS

"...and loving be natural as breathing and warm as sunlight..."

(A. S. J. Tessimond)

As I started secondary school in the 1950s Alan Turing was being chemically castrated. His crime? The Love that dares not speak its name. During the last half century there has been a social and cultural revolution in public attitudes to inclusion and integrity. The LGBT (Lesbian Gay Bisexual and Transgender) community has seen a seismic shift in public policy towards gay women and men. As HM the Queen apparently said on signing the Equal Marriage Act into law: "Whoever would have believed at the time of my coronation that I would be signing this today." That may or may not be an urban myth but it sums up the revolution in thought and action that has been the foundation of the fulfilment that I feel today.

But that reality is not shared by millions of gay people across the world. Violent hostility and death threats to gay people persist in countries as diverse as Russia and Nigeria. It is impossible to be openly gay in countless countries and equal marriage would just be a fantasy in many societies. Chemical castration is still practised in some of them. Even in Europe and the USA the rise of far right movements and bonkers politicians threatens to undermine the fragile rights gained in the last half century. The freedoms that gay people now enjoy in some societies are the direct result of the sexual and cultural revolutions that took place in the mid twentieth century. Those revolutions gave birth to campaign groups like Stonewall, the Campaign for Homosexual Equality, the Terence Higgins Campaign and the Gay Christian Movement. They all worked fearlessly for the liberation of the LGBT community.

That inheritance needs to be used now to further the cause of LGBT people in other parts of the world. There are pressures within that community that work against any form of community engagement. The magazines that feed the male gay community are often obsessed with physical appearance: the "beautiful boy" still persists as the dominant icon. That tendency is exacerbated by the cult of celebrity and the hidden demand for beautiful men, straight or gay, to be icons in film and theatre and art. All of that blunts the political will to engage on the international stage with the radical issues of justice faced by gay sisters and brothers in other cultures. If there is an Achilles Heel in the gay community it is a tendency towards self-obsession and "selfies". The film "Pride" highlighted the power that can be released when people from different cultures…in this case the mining and gay communities…collaborate in forging new political alliances. That same energy needs releasing again in relation to international issues of sexuality and justice.

A similar energy was released in the USA, and then in Europe, in the 1980s when the scourge of AIDS surfaced. My friend, David, was one of the first victims. I well remember going to see him in a South London hospital and the battle that transpired between me and the hospital staff about the need to wear the kind of protective clothing that workmen use for the removal of lethal asbestos! I won! But the fight in the USA and Europe was on a much bigger scale. The gay community in New York and San Francisco had to mobilise to persuade federal and national governments that resources needed to be released for scientific and medical research into the causes of the disease. That mobilised the gay community in a way that nothing else has. That is not to diminish the tragedy of thousands of deaths in the USA and Europe or the millions that have died and continue to die from the illness in Africa and other developing countries. If there is one good thing that has emerged from the destructive illness it is the energy that gay people found to work for the human rights of their fellow human beings.

The shadow that AIDS cast over diverse communities had another important effect. It confronted gay men in particular with issues about their lifestyle and the questions those issues raised about relationships and the part that sex plays in the shaping of human identity. Gay men like to dodge questions about sexual promiscuity and multiple sexual relationships. AIDS forced the questions about safe sex and what really makes for fulfilment in life. The questions could not be dodged anymore. The gay community does not bear the sole brunt for the sexual practices that had developed. The wider community, certainly in the United Kingdom, has to take responsibility as well. The criminalisation of homosexuality forced men into underground and hidden activity. It is not a step too far from that for sex to become "a dirty little secret". Public policy in the UK up until 1967 forced thousands of men into inappropriate relationships. It played havoc with their sense of self-esteem and their grasp of human integrity. In some cases, and not least within the British churches, it created a misogynistic culture that held back the freedom of women for generations.

The issue of gay or equal marriage has again brought the issues of sexuality and religious freedom to the fore again. For my generation it is an ambivalent issue. I am passionately in favour of equal human rights and especially the right of human beings to embrace relationships that bring fulfilment and hope. Nevertheless I grew up in a culture where the understanding of marriage has been determined by centuries of Western culture. I find it difficult to escape from the mental construct that marriage is between a man and a woman. I rejoiced when the UK introduced the notion of civil partnerships and Ralph and I embraced that with all the Joie de vivre we could muster. It was one of the most joyous days of our lives. We will never forget the rapturous applause that greeted us as we entered Deal Town Hall. Even the Town Sergeant said that he had never felt the place filled with so much Love as at that moment. I am left wondering what equal marriage could add to that. The key can only lie in the right of human beings to have equality before the Law. But that is a legal rather than a spiritual matter…or is it?

As I have grappled to understand "the varieties of myself" in the course of this book and why I have lived a life both in and out of the Church the question of human sexuality and spirituality has been inescapable. I know it is no longer an issue for millions of people in Britain today and in that sense this book will be irrelevant to them. Nevertheless I want to press the questions because I believe that they are of vital contemporary relevance to some of the hard questions that our society faces. In my lifetime the spotlight has been shone on aberrations of sexual behaviour that are truly horrific. Whether it is the Saville case in the BBC or the sexual malpractices of Roman Catholic priests in the USA and Ireland or the criminal cases of sexual abuse by Church of England priests in pockets of the Church of England in West Sussex and London, we are aware that the dislocation of human sexuality and religious practice can be lethal. The stories of the victims of sexual abuse by priests, bishops and monks are a horrifying stain on a civilised society. The "turning of the blind eye" by the media and religious authorities is equally obscene and destructive of a compassionate community.

There is no doubt in my mind that the Church's attitude to homosexuality lays close to the roots of this abusive behaviour. If an institution causes women and men to live a life of hidden sexual repression there are bound to be consequences. In my experience in parts of the Church of England that is covered up with a camp attitude towards religious behaviour and elaborate dressing up. I have not the slightest doubt that the behaviour of a prince bishop in West Sussex for many years contributed to the sexual abuse practised by a few priests. This public practice of institutional homophobia leads directly to sexual malpractice and a lifetime of human suffering. This is no less true of public institutions like the BBC where enquiries have shown that the cult of celebrity led senior managers to ignore every warning they received about sexual abuse.

That is why I believe that the dislocation of sexuality and spirituality is of fundamental importance for our health as a society. It also goes to the heart of what I believe spirituality is about. For me it is the fulfilment of our humanity. That is why I cannot understand the opposition of the churches to equal marriage. Marriage or spiritual partnership is about taking the root meaning of our humanity into a universal Love. If the person of Jesus means anything to me that is what it is? He is the icon of human and universal love integrated in a single being. That is an unfashionable position to take both in contemporary society and in the contemporary churches. But what confronting my own gay sexuality has taught me is this: it has brought together issues of international justice and health, compassion and the stand against human abuse, the meanings of integrity and authenticity, the issues around public policy and political engagement and helped me to see all that in a holistic way. It has enabled me to find wholeness and yet to go on living forwards, not complacent that "the best is yet to come".

From my early sexual fumbling in the bluebell woods of rural Suffolk with adolescent boyfriends to the mature sexual relationship that I enjoy with Ralph, my gay sexual identity has been at the root of all that I am. It caused me such acute pain whilst I tried to be a good priest that it propelled me to seek a different life. There are many who would say that I should have stayed within the institution and made the sacrifice of fighting for the rights of LGBT people within that Church. There are a few who do that and they have my unlimited admiration. But we are all different. If I had stayed I am certain that I would have some form of breakdown and as a consequence would have had little effect. Living outside the Church has made me no less human. In the community where I now live it has probably been a contribution to "welcoming the stranger", to enriching a community where gay women and men are embraced for who they are. That is both a personal and a political statement: it is a small victory, a small act of defiance to those across the world who would put me to death if they had the chance! Glad rags and handbags are the symbols of my defiance!

CHAPTER NINE

THE LIVING YEARS

"...we are, each of us, the accretion of all that we have been."

(Penelope Lively)

The Mike and the Mechanics song *The Living Years* is almost a ballad for the men of my generation. We are possibly the last generation to suffer from that lack of emotional bonding with our fathers that characterised men traumatised by both the First and Second World Wars. The regret and loss that the song captures so vividly is also perhaps an anthem for the loss of identity that afflicted Britain for much of the twentieth century; it is a story of lost empires and a more personal story about the loss of emotional security that comes with distant relationships. Yet despite all that as I face the last decades of my life I am also struck by how much like my father I am. Through the emotional silence he gave me a number of gifts, of which a passion and love for the natural world is one. Life was to be celebrated in all its vibrancy. It was to be grasped and lived at the boundaries of our talent and natural horizons. In that sense he represented a generation that was also pushing at those boundaries, even to the Moon, Mars and beyond.

It is that boundless exploration that does not sit comfortably with the emergence of the later years of life. Suddenly you are aware of the limitations when the synchronicity of the body starts to fail. Memory plays its tricks and you are all too aware the people living with the hell of Alzheimer's or dementia are not far away. If this is a crisis for my generation it will be an even more profound one for the Ziggy Stardust generation. It may be an intolerable burden to accept a life where there are boundaries and limitations. But in all this there is a deeper irony and a potential opportunity. Those of us entering the final decades of life now have the chance to be pioneers, pioneers of a new way of growing old. Our lives have equipped us well for that. Britain has seen a huge surge in innovation and entrepreneurial skills in the decades after the Second World War. We are a nation of inventors and we need to adapt that skill to the ways in which we live together. Medical advances have been so dramatic that phrases like "seventy is the new fifty" easily trip off our lips.

We are accustomed to certain ways of looking and being shaped by social, medical and cultural advances that are breathtaking. We need to charge those accustomed ways of thought with new significance. A pioneer feels a sharpened and new sense of pleasure in the world around us. She, or he, can luxuriate in a deeper appreciation of the world we live in. Of course that can be blunted by ill health but we also need to grasp that the people growing older in Britain today also have a surer grasp of health, and what makes us healthy, than previous generations could ever have dreamt of. We also have the capacity to dream of new ways of living and being together. We will not tolerate what has passed for care of the elderly in the past and we are going to fight for much more joined-up thinking about health and care in the final decades of living. I have no wish to finish up in a gay ghetto of old men. But nor do I want to end my days isolated and alone because I cannot express myself with freedom and celebration.

This sense of sharpened pleasure in the world around came through one of the gifts that my father, and his father, gave me. It was the love of plants and a passion for gardening. Again there is irony here. Gardening is always about the anticipation of the future. You are always looking forward. Whether it is the intense joy I experienced this morning as I saw the first primroses on the slopes of the common as I walked the dogs or the anticipation of the first new potatoes on the allotment or the planning of a recreation of the bottom half of my garden, anticipation runs through it all. Penelope Lively writes:

"the miraculous power of gardening – it evokes tomorrow, it is forward looking, it invites plans and expectations, creativity, ambitions."

That anticipation of tomorrow is at the heart of it all but a shadow also falls across it: the reality that it has to be squared with the prospect of dying. As the son of a funeral director and half a lifetime as a priest death has been the familiar companion for most of my life. I know all too well how it diminishes people and those close to them. I have seen potential wasted and tragedy stalk and diminish the lives of many people. But alongside that have been people dying with a dignity and grace that glorifies everything that is meant by being human. The difference is often about being in the right place at the right time.

At its simplest level gardening puts you in touch with the exhilaration of life, with the rhythm of the seasons and with power of growth. But every gardener knows that in order for plants to thrive it is all a case of 'right plant, right place'. Plants need different conditions in which to thrive. A shade-loving fern is not going to thrive in a place that gets the full sun all day long. A sunflower will fade away very fast under a woodland glade. This is no less true of people. Part of my own liberation was doing a Myers Briggs test in my counselling training. I finally confronted that I fall well over the Introspection side of the human spectrum. I am anything but a party animal. In fact they make me intensely anxious. Ralph, my partner, on the other hand revels in high amounts of social contact and blossoms when he is performing as Miss Pussy D'Amour! Yet somehow fire and water together, introspective and extrovert, has created nearly thirty years of glorious partnership. My grandfather, a 'Dig for Britain' veteran, taught me first how to grow vegetables, the different conditions of soil and the nutrients required for good results. My father took up the baton first of all by surrounding our council house garden with Leylandii trees, a disastrous and expensive mistake. But he then changed to rose trees and grew specimens that finished up on the show benches of the national rose shows in London. From both of them I learnt this essential truth: people and plants are the same. They both need the right conditions to grow into their true selves. We flourish and are fulfilled when we are in the right place.

This passion for gardening landed me on the national stage, a place that was uncomfortable for me to be. In 2000 the shop staff decided that they would nominate me for the BBC Gardener of the Year competition. It was not a good time. I was dealing with the planning battles that I described in an earlier chapter. I was mentally exhausted and had very little physical energy. But I was caught. I loved my garden in Worcester Park in London. It opened each year for the National Gardens Scheme and hundreds of people had visited it. More than one national newspaper and garden magazine had shown an interest in it. That, at least, redeemed them in my eyes. It was not the *Sun* and the *News of the World* hounding me around London! The BBC first of all sprung a fifty-question quiz on me over the phone and followed it up with judges visiting the garden. Apparently I got 19/20 on the first round. So it was off to Birmingham for four days to create a garden from scratch. Scratch it was: an area of soil full of old toilet paper, broken glass and builders' rubble! The other five contestants were great people and we all bonded with a common passion for gardening. That sent Diarmuid Gavin, the presenter, and the production team into overdrive. They did everything possible to force us apart. They failed!

In the end I was the runner-up, missing the top prize by a couple of points. It felt like being the underdog once again but it turned out to be a "desired difficulty". Gardening is also the victim of celebrity cults and gardening celebrities can be like celebrity chefs, shouting the virtues of garden makeovers and home-cooked meals but not actually changing the landscape or the dining tables of Britain. Taking part in the programme brought me in touch with hundreds of people passionate about the skills of gardening and equally passionate about sharing them with others. Organisations like the National Gardens Scheme create huge networks of people ready to share their acquired knowledge and skills with others. It is as opposed to a celebrity cult as anything could be. Instead it is a democracy of anticipation and reciprocity combined with a generosity of spirit often sadly lacking in many communities.

From a small boy helping his grandfather in his vegetable garden to appearing on national gardening programmes, from being a flower-arranging teenager to organising flower festivals in churches and cathedrals, this passion has been one of the cores of my life. It has also been a vital part of my physical and emotional health. When I faced my true self in 1980 and realised that my marriage could not work I went into a very deep depression. My worth as a person seemed to be at stake. First of all I tried medication but the anti-depressants very quickly finished up in a rubbish bin in the Waterloo underpass. For the next five years I entered a period of Jungian psychotherapy. It was a strange and private world. I was already convinced that there was an intangible link between depression and grief and loss. To the therapist much of my rambling must have sounded like *The Living Years* stuck in a groove from which there was no escape. But that, of course, is why the song has such a powerful hold on my emotions. I explored the demons and the dragons that haunted my imagination. In fact one session will always live with me. I battled with a ferocious dragon for fifty minutes leaving the therapy room as exhausted as I have ever felt in my whole life. It took me sixty minutes to do a walk that normally would take ten.

The therapy led to a strange kind of growth. It was as though I had hit rock bottom but, in finding the bottom, had also discovered the foundation of my life. In many ways it paralleled the experience of gardening, clearing the weeds and tumbleweed of half a life, nurturing the soil and finding the right place for me. As well as valuing the insights of Jung and the ambiguous path of therapy I rediscovered the therapeutic value of gardening and the central role it has played in my life. In the last twenty years that discovery has become much more common. Scented gardens for people with visual disability, the power of gardening in prisoner rehabilitation, the use of gardening therapy in the treatment of mental illness: all those are indicative of the power of plants to heal, the endless possibilities of the natural world. Today my allotment and garden are welcome refuges from the endless demands that people make on me "to do something about IT"! They suit my introspective nature and nurture that soul that tries "never to neglect the forests and the oceans".

Part of the ageing process is about holding the contradictions together. The anticipation of the future and the horizon of death form the landscape in which the last decades must be lived. Feeling the vibrancy of life whilst preparing for the limitations that age inevitably brings. Kate Gross in *Late Fragment* celebrates the intensity of friendship, partnership, companionship even in the face of incurable illness. She celebrates *The Living Years* even as she faces the inevitability of death from a hideous form of cancer. It is a gift from another generation to my generation. It is almost a charge to celebrate all the possibilities of life whilst not being deluded that they consist in endless party going and a large cocaine and alcohol intake. It is a forward-looking celebration, not regretting that she will have no part of her children's and partner's future, but urging them towards that tomorrow which writes plans and visions even when the human landscape has changed.

In the second half of my life I have been blessed with a quality of emotional and physical health that I could not have dreamt of in the first half. The gardens that Ralph and I have created have been outward symbols of an inner relationship that has nurtured us both through three decades. My abiding friendship with my two daughters has irrigated the wellsprings of my humanity. When they reached university age I told them "Parents have to turn into friends". That has been my aspiration and I hope it has had some truth for them. Their acceptance of Ralph's and my partnership has certainly nourished us. To some the eighteen years that separates Ralph and me might appear to be a hindrance, even a disability. For me he is at the heart of my vitality, my hopes that the future can still be a thrill, the luxury of appreciating the world that I still inhabit. He never stops challenging me to be that person that I am capable of being. Without his nagging this book would never have been written! I hope in turn that our partnership has sustained him through family trauma, career disruption and emotional abandonment. I know our civil partnership, our joyous acceptance of our gay destiny and our embracing of many different kinds of people has been an inspiration to others. They truly have been *The Living Years*.

POSTSCRIPT

"Before being Christians or Jews or Muslims, before being Americans or Russians or Africans, before being generals or priests, rabbis or imams, before having visible or invisible disabilities, we are all human beings with hearts capable of loving." (Jean Vanier on accepting the Templeton Prize 2015)

My exploration of a life lived inside and outside of the Church began with a search for "the varieties of himself" (Sir Thomas Browne) Through the roads not taken, the mistakes made and the ambiguities lived through I have tried to discover something of the inner meaning of my life. A lot of that has been mundane, lived far away from the cult of celebrity that dominates Western culture at the beginning of the twenty-first century. I have told the story not least because I wanted to set on record what it was like trying to live life as a gay man with profound spiritual needs at a time when the churches of Britain could not reconcile their doctrine with this dimension of being human. It is a story that needs to be told.

But there is a deeper dimension to it than that. I wanted to set the record straight. Churches often claimed that gay people are less than fulfilled. A former Archbishop of Canterbury, Robert Runcie, called us disabled. I hope my story exposed that as a lie. I would like to feel that my experience is one of embodied hope. Of course I have lived with that disconcerting muddle of what I intended to happen and what actually took place. But I have also tried to see it as some kind of whole. I believe passionately in seeing others holistically. I cannot escape the same scrutiny. There will be perversity in that but in shedding all the labels by which we define ourselves, by letting go of the roles I have performed, I can find my final happiness in "a heart capable of loving" and a life lived in the victory of Hope.

What then do I make of the foundation stone on which the struggle has been lived and some of the difficulties overcome? Through it all there has been an inescapable truth that has never let me go. It is the conviction that at the very heart of my being I am loved. That love has been mediated to me through a multitude of people of many races and many different backgrounds. They are a glorious ragbag of humanity. My daughters' acceptance of me is a gift without price. I dedicate this book to them. For the last thirty years Ralph has been my rock: without him I would be a greatly diminished person. Instead I feel wonderfully loved and fulfilled. I have told the story of yesterday not out of any kind of nostalgia. It has been a labour of love in the interests of tomorrow.

NOTES

There are two books to which I have been especially indebted in writing this book. Both of them are exceptional memoirs with a character so different to conventional autobiography:

Penelope Lively: *Ammonites and Leaping Fish* (Penguin 2014)
Kate Gross: *Late Fragments* (Collins 2015)

For the historical background to Chapter one I am indebted to:
Sarah Mars: *The Politics of Addiction* (Palgrave Macmillan)

For the chapter titles I have used or gently adapted the following:
Dark Side of the Moon (Pink Floyd 1973)
Stranger on the Shore (Acker Bilk 1961)
The Man with the Child in his Eyes (Kate Bush 1978)
What Becomes of the Broken Hearted (Jimmy Ruffin 1966)
Fields of Gold (Sting 1993)
Shopping (Pet Shop Boys on album Actually 1987)

I Will Survive (Perren and Fekaris 1978)
Handbags and Gladrags (Mike d'Abo 1967)
The Living Years (Mike and the Mechanics 1988)

For the inspiration and the emotional rollercoaster those
songs have provided, thanks.